PICTURE GRAPHS

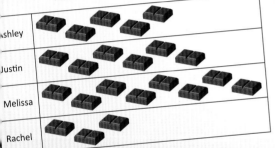

Number of chocolate bars sold

ashley	
Justin	
Melissa	
Rachel	

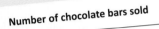

KEY: Each

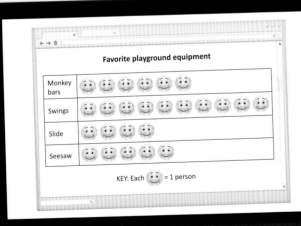

Favorite playground equipment

Monkey bars	
Swings	
Slide	
Seesaw	

KEY: Each = 1 person

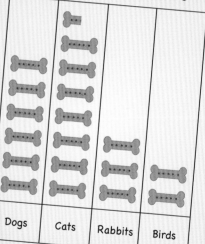

Number of animals on Nov. 5

| Dogs | Cats | Rabbits | Birds |

KEY: Each = 2 animals

Crystal Sikkens

Crabtree Publishing Company

www.crabtreebooks.com

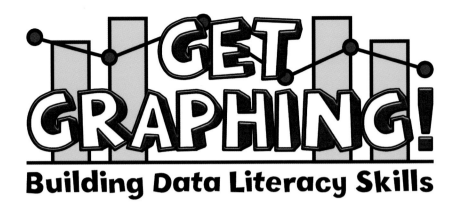

Building Data Literacy Skills

Author: Crystal Sikkens

Series research and development:
Reagan Miller

Editorial director: Kathy Middleton

Photo research: Crystal Sikkens,
Katherine Berti

Design: Katherine Berti

Proofreader: Janine Deschenes

Indexer: Petrice Custance

Print and production coordinator:
Katherine Berti

Image credits:
Thinkstock: p 14 (left); p 21
All other images by Shutterstock

Library and Archives Canada Cataloguing in Publication

Sikkens, Crystal, author
          Picture graphs / Crystal Sikkens.

(Get graphing! Building data literacy skills)
Includes index.
Issued in print and electronic formats.
ISBN 978-0-7787-2632-6 (hardback).--
ISBN 978-0-7787-2636-4 (paperback)
ISBN 978-1-4271-1839-4 (html)

          1. Graphic methods--Juvenile literature. 2. Charts, diagrams, etc.--
Juvenile literature. 3. Mathematics--Charts, diagrams, etc.--Juvenile
literature. I. Title.

QA90.S546 2016   j518'.23   C2016-903319-8
                                                    C2016-903320-1

Library of Congress Cataloging-in-Publication Data

CIP available at the Library of Congress

Crabtree Publishing Company
www.crabtreebooks.com   1-800-387-7650

Printed in Canada/022016/IH20151223

Published in Canada
Crabtree Publishing
616 Welland Ave.
St. Catharines, Ontario
L2M 5V6

Published in the United States
Crabtree Publishing
PMB 59051
350 Fifth Avenue, 59th Floor
New York, New York 10118

Published in the United Kingdom
Crabtree Publishing
Maritime House
Basin Road North, Hove
BN41 1WR

Published in Australi
Crabtree Publishing
3 Charles Street
Coburg North
VIC 3058

Contents

Sharing Information

Data is a collection of information. People share data through numbers, words, photographs, or drawings. In today's world we have data all around us. Turning on the TV, surfing the Internet, or picking up a newspaper or book are quick and easy ways to find data.

Baseball scores and weather reports are examples of data that can be found on the Internet.

Number of chocolate bars sold

Ashley	
Justin	
Melissa	
Rachel	

KEY:
Each 🍫 = 1 chocolate bar

*Graphs make it easier to **compare** information or track changes over time.*

Graphs and Charts

People share data in different ways.
One way people share data is by making
graphs or charts. Graphs use lines, shapes,
and colors to sort and organize data.
Graphs are useful because they show
data in a way that is easy to understand.

Different Graphs

There are many different kinds of graphs. Bar graphs, line graphs, and picture graphs are the most common kinds. Each kind of graph is used to show different types of information.

Bar graphs use colored bars to compare information or show larger changes over time.

Line graphs use points and lines to show small changes over a period of time.

Picture Graphs

This book will teach you all about picture graphs. Picture graphs are also called pictographs. Like bar graphs, they are used to compare information. However, instead of using bars to show the data, picture graphs use pictures.

Number of fish caught on camping trip

Dad	🐟🐟🐟🐟🐟🐟
Jeremy	🐟🐟🐟🐟
Teresa	🐟🐟🐟🐟🐟🐟🐟
Mom	🐟🐟

KEY: Each 🐟 = 1 fish

The same data can be shown in both a bar graph and a picture graph.

Picture Graph Parts

All picture graphs include the same main parts. Each part has an important purpose that helps the reader understand the graph. Once you know the parts, you will be able to create your own picture graphs!

The **category labels** let readers know what is being compared.

The **title** tells readers what information is being shown on the graph.

Favorite playground equipment

Monkey bars	😊 😊 😊 😊 😊 😊
Swings	😊 😊 😊 😊 😊 😊 😊 😊 😊 😊
Slide	😊 😊 😊 😊
Seesaw	😊 😊 😊 😊 😊

KEY: Each 😊 = 1 person

The **pictures** or **symbols** show the data that was collected. One symbol equals a specific number.

The **key** shows the value or number of items each picture represents.

Be a Data Detective!

Why are the pictures an important part of a picture graph?

A Key Part

To make a picture graph clear and easy to read, it is best to use 10 or less pictures on the graph. If your data includes numbers larger than 10, you can make the pictures represent more than one item. You list the number of items each picture represents in the key.

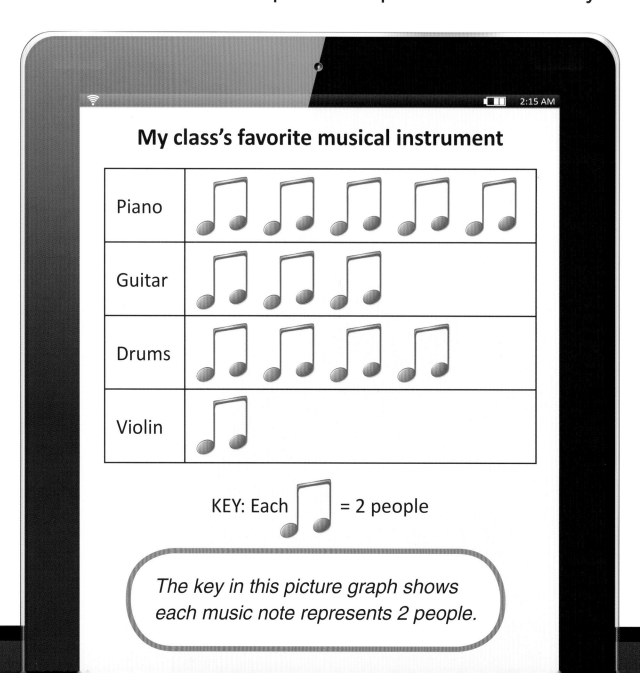

The key in this picture graph shows each music note represents 2 people.

Half Amounts

Some picture graphs might show how half of a picture. This is used when a data amount is half of the key amount. For example, if only one person voted for violin as their favorite instrument, you could use ♪ to represent one person on the graph on page 10.

Be a Data Detective!

Look at the two picture graphs below. Which one shows that Julie picked 15 apples? Remember to check the key!

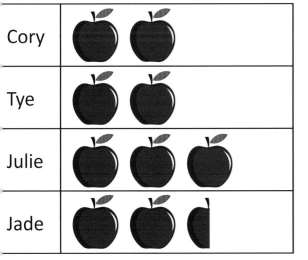

Number of apples picked in one hour

Cory	🍎🍎
Tye	🍎🍎
Julie	🍎🍎🍎
Jade	🍎🍎🍎

KEY: Each 🍎 = 10 apples

Number of apples picked in one hour

Cory	🍎🍎
Tye	🍎🍎
Julie	🍎🍎🍎
Jade	🍎🍎

KEY: Each 🍎 = 5 apples

Same and Different

Picture graphs can show the same data in two different ways. The data can be displayed either **vertically** or **horizontally**. On a horizontal picture graph the pictures are drawn in rows. The pictures on a vertical picture graph are drawn in columns.

The pictures on a horizontal picture graph are drawn side by side, starting on the left.

Flowers in my garden

Tulips				
Roses				
Daisies				
Lilies				

KEY: Each = 3 flowers

Category Labels

The category labels on a vertical picture graph are found at the bottom of the graph. Horizontal picture graphs have the labels on the left side. There is usually more room to fit longer category labels on a horizontal picture graph.

The pictures on a vertical picture graph are stacked one on top of the other.

Be a Data Detective!

List the kinds of flowers from most to least using either the horizontal or vertical picture graph.

Flowers in my garden

Tulips	Roses	Daisies	Lilies

KEY: Each = 3 flowers

Counting Animals

Sophie helps out at the local animal shelter every Saturday. When she arrives each week she counts all the animals, then puts the data into a picture graph. This helps the shelter know how many animals have come and gone over the week.

Need a Good Home!

Tally Charts

Each week, Sophie begins by creating a **tally chart**. A tally chart is a table with **tally marks** that shows a set of data. As she counts each animal, she makes one tally mark on the tally chart. Once she is done, she will use the data to create her picture graph.

> Tally marks are easier to count if they are organized into groups of five.

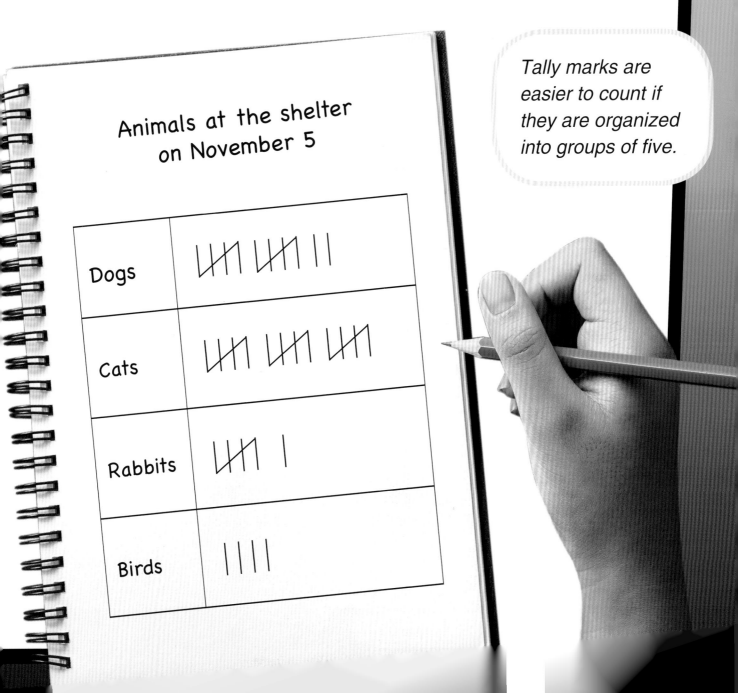

Animals at the shelter on November 5

Dogs	卌 卌		
Cats	卌 卌 卌
Rabbits	卌	
Birds	|||||

Creating a Graph

Sophie creates a vertical picture graph using the data she has collected. She first makes a table with columns for each kind of animal. Then she adds category labels at the bottom of each column and a title at the top that includes the date.

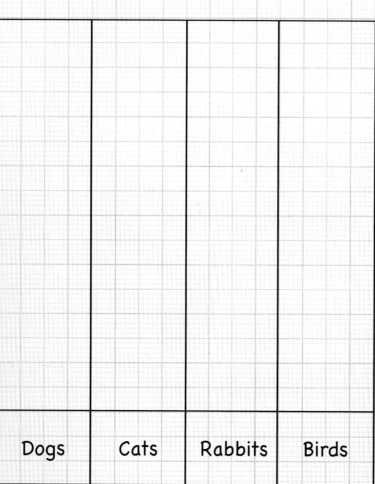

Animals at the shelter
on November 5

Dogs	Cats	Rabbits	Birds

Finding the Key

Sophie must decide on a key for the graph. She looks at her tally chart. She sees some rows have more than 10 tally marks, but less than 20. She decides that making each picture on her graph represent two animals will be the easiest to read.

Sophie decides to use a dog treat as the symbol on her graph. She shows the amount the symbol represents in the key.

Animals at the shelter on November 5

Dogs	Cats	Rabbits	Birds

KEY: Each 🦴 = 2 animals

Adding the Data

Sophie's next step is to add the data to her graph. For every two tally marks on her tally chart, Sophie draws one dog treat. For the rows on her tally chart that have one tally mark left over, she draws half of a dog treat to represent one.

Sophie made all the pictures on her graph the same size and the same distance apart. This makes the data easier to read.

Animals at the shelter on November 5

(graph with columns labeled)

Dogs | Cats | Rabbits | Birds

KEY: Each 🦴 = 2 animals

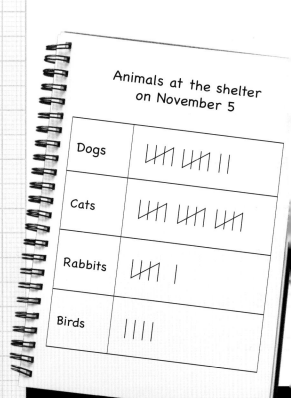

Animals at the shelter on November 5

Dogs	𝄺𝄺 𝄺𝄺 𝄺𝄺 𝄺𝄺 𝄺𝄺 𝄺 𝄺
Cats	𝄺𝄺 𝄺𝄺 𝄺𝄺
Rabbits	𝄺𝄺 𝄺
Birds	𝄺𝄺𝄺𝄺

T-charts

A **T-chart** helps you organize data on a picture graph. It is a good tool to use when you have to answer questions about a graph where the key is more than one. A T-chart can be made by simply drawing a capital "T." On the left side of the vertical line, you write numbers in a column starting with one. These numbers represent the number of pictures on the graph. On the right side, you write the values, or amounts of the pictures based on the key.

Be a Data Detective!

Use Sophie's graph to answer the below questions. You can use the T-chart on this page to help you.

1. How many more cats are in the shelter than dogs?

2. What is the total number of rabbits and birds?

1	2
2	4
3	6
4	8
5	10
6	12
7	14
8	16

Collecting New Data

Sophie missed a week at the shelter. Mrs. Blackburn, the owner of the animal shelter, counted the animals instead. She gave Sophie a tally chart with the data and asked her to create another picture graph. They will then compare last week's graph to this week's to see which week had the most animals in the shelter.

Animals at the shelter on November 11	
Dogs	卌 卌 IIII
Cats	卌 卌 卌 IIII
Rabbits	卌
Birds	IIII

Now it's Your Turn!

Help Sophie by creating a picture graph using the data on Mrs. Blackburn's tally chart. You can use the checklist on the right to help you.

Remember to make sure you have all these parts on your graph:

✔ title
✔ category labels
✔ key
✔ pictures

Need a Good Home!

Comparing the Data

Be a Data Detective!

Use the two picture graphs on this page to answer the questions below.

1. What is the total number of animals on each graph?

2. a) Was there more animals in the shelter on Nov. 5 or Nov. 11?
   b) What was the difference?

Number of animals on Nov. 5

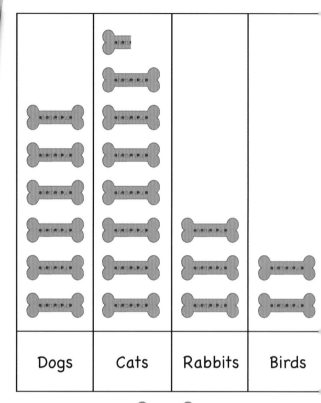

Dogs	Cats	Rabbits	Birds

KEY: Each 🦴 = 2 animals

Number of animals on Nov. 11

Dogs	🦴🦴🦴🦴🦴🦴🦴
Cats	🦴🦴🦴🦴🦴🦴🦴🦴🦴🦴🦴
Rabbits	🦴🦴🦴
Birds	🦴🦴

KEY: Each 🦴 = 2 animals

Learning More

Books

Cocca, Lisa Colozza. *Pictographs* (Making and Using Graphs). Cherry Lake Publishing, 2014.

Nelson, Robin. *Let's Make a Picture Graph*. Lerner Publishing Group, 2012.

Piddock, Claire. *Line, Bar, and Circle Graphs* (My Path to Math). Crabtree Publishing Company, 2010.

Websites

Review what you have learned about picture graphs and then take a quiz to test what you know at:
www.mathsisfun.com/data/pictographs.html

Take a quiz and test your knowledge of pictographs at:
https://ca.ixl.com/math/grade-3/interpret-pictographs

Have fun making picture graphs by playing this game:
https://ca.ixl.com/math/grade-2/create-pictographs

Get Graphing Online!

You can also create graphs online! The link below has a list of websites that let you type in your data to create your own graphs. Most of these websites let you print or save your graph when you are finished. You can begin by making different bar graphs using the data found in this book.

http://interactivesites. weebly.com/graphing.html

About the Author

Crystal Sikkens has been working at Crabtree Publishing for over 15 years. She has helped write, edit, and find pictures for many of Crabtree's titles, including *Measure it!*, *Engineers Solve Problems*, and *Length Word Problems*. When Crystal's not creating books, she enjoys spending time on the family farm with her husband John and daughter Hailey.

Glossary

Note: Some boldfaced words are defined where they appear in the text.

compare To find out how things are similar or different

data Information that is gathered or collected

horizontally To be flat or straight across

tally chart A way to show data using tally marks in a table

tally mark A vertical or diagonal line used for counting

T-chart A type of picture graph used to organize data

vertically Positioned straight up and down

Index

Answers

Page 9: The pictures show the amount of data in each category.
Page 11: B
Page 13: Tulips, Lilies, Daisies, Roses
Page 19: 1) 3
2) 10

Pages 22:
1) Nov. 5 = 37
Nov. 11 = 40
2) a. Nov. 11
b. 3